Great Scientific
Questions and the
Scientists Who
Answered Them™

HOW DO WE KNOW

HOW THE
BRAIN WORKS

DONALD CLEVELAND

Great Scientific Questions and the Scientists Who Answered Them™

HOW DO WE KNOW
HOW THE BRAIN WORKS

THE ROSEN PUBLISHING GROUP, INC.
NEW YORK

Published in 2005 by The Rosen Publishing Group, Inc.
29 East 21st Street, New York, NY 10010

Copyright © 2005 by The Rosen Publishing Group, Inc.

First Edition

Library of Congress Cataloging-in-Publication Data

Cleveland, Don, 1935–
How do we know how the brain works/Don Cleveland.—1st ed.
        p. cm.—(Great scientific questions and the scientists who answered them)
Includes bibliographical references and index.
Contents: What is a mind?—About neuroscience—Theories in psychology—
The world of cognitive science—New technologies in brain processes
ISBN 1-4042-0078-9 (library binding)
1. Brain—Juvenile literature. 2. Neuroscience—Juvenile literature.
3. Psychology—Juvenile literature. 4. Cognitive science—Juvenile literature.
[1. Brain. 2. Neuroscience. 3. Cognitive science. 4. Psychology.]
I. Title. II. Series.
QP376.C56 2005
153—dc22

                                                                    2003024419

Manufactured in the United States of America

Cover: Magnetic resonance imaging of a person's head.
Cover inset: The human brain.

Contents

What Is a Mind?

What are you doing right now? Obviously, you are reading the first paragraph of this book. How do you know that this is what you are doing in the first place? Who are you and how do you know for sure that you are you and not somebody else?

Silly questions? Not in the least. It is your brain that is figuring out what you are doing, and

it is your mind, your consciousness, your feeling of self-awareness, that knows who you are. Your mind is telling you that you are a "self" and is reassuring you that you know very well who that self is. Your senses feel your body, but not other bodies, giving you an idea of your separateness from the rest of the world. Because of your mind, nobody else in the entire world is exactly like you. You are unique.

The human brain and the mind it generates is one of the most amazing and remarkable wonders in all of nature. In the pages that follow, we will look at what we know about the mind and what we still don't know. We will meet some of the major players in the quest to understand how the brain works and what this means to us.

Trying to figure out how the brain/mind works is a valiant adventure. What we have here is not a simple kitchen device, like a toaster, but a complex biological organ, which works by initiating and controlling billions of chemical and electrical operations. In order to

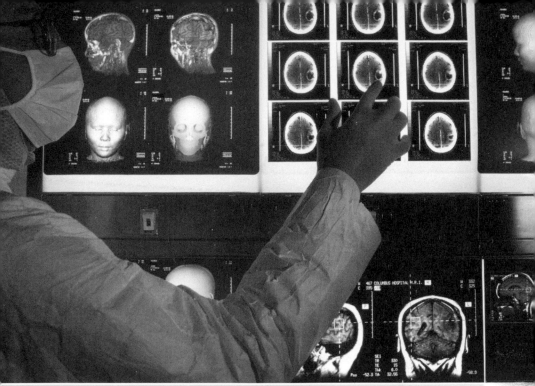

A doctor examines magnetic resonance images (MRIs) taken from different angles of the patient's head. This technology allows specialists the ability to tailor an exam to a specific medical question being asked.

understand ourselves we have to understand how these electrochemical operations come together to make us who we are. Why and how the brain does this is determined by both our genetic inheritance and the physical and cultural environment we live in.

Over the years, countless scientists have spent a great part of their lives trying to answer questions about the mind and where it came from. Many of these scientists are famous and many are not remembered. Let's begin our story by stepping a long way back into history for a moment.

WHAT THE ANCIENTS THOUGHT

The brain has interested us since our species evolved and we became human. At archaeological sites more than 10,000 years old, we have found human skulls with holes drilled in them. This practice of drilling holes in the skull is called "trepanning." Our ancestors might have been trying to fix a malfunctioning brain or perhaps letting out "bad spirits." It is likely that early people knew that when somebody's head got bashed, it brought on ill effects. The victim might have passed out, started jerking, lost his memory, or had other symptoms. They probably noticed that the victim's behavior or perception of his or her surroundings changed. They knew that functions take place in the head and that they sometimes go awry.

When humans began to write, they left us some important documents related to the brain, usually in a medical context. One of the earliest of these, known as the Edwin Smith papyrus, was written around 1600 BC in Egypt. This was a medical account of forty-eight clinical cases of head and spine trauma. These case studies make it clear that early doctors understood that brain injuries could cause changes in functions throughout the body.

Alcmaeon of Croton, who was born around 535 BC, pointed out that the brain is the site of sensations. For example, when a mosquito bites you, it's your brain that tells you about it in no uncertain terms. Democritus (460–370 BC), Diogenes (400–325 BC), Plato (427–347 BC), and others all thought that the brain controlled the activities of the body. Aristotle (384–322 BC), however, thought such activities were controlled by the heart.

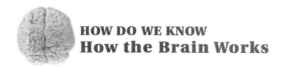

Hippocrates (460–400 BC) thought that the brain makes all emotions and activities possible. Herophilus (335–280 BC), often called the father of scientific anatomy, dissected brains and described their cavities, which we now call cerebral ventricles, and proposed that the cavities were related to mental functions.

During the Middle Ages, scholars generally reiterated ideas from classical times and then did some speculating of their own. For example, they added the idea that spirits wander in the cavities of the brain. The Renaissance ushered in a new dimension of thinking about the brain. The Belgian anatomist Andreas Vesalius (1514–1564), considered the father of modern anatomy, still believed that spirits floated around in the brain, but he didn't believe that mental skills lay in the brain cavities.

René Descartes (1596–1650) put forward the idea that our brains have something important to do with our behavior. Some of his ideas about the brain were eccentric, such as the concept that animal spirits move

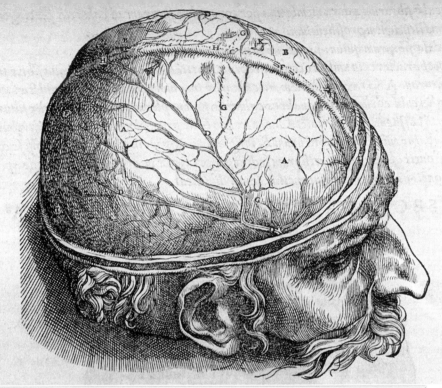

This anatomical diagram of the fibrous membrane surrounding the human brain is an illustration by Andreas Vesalius from a seven-volume text, published in 1543. This revolutionary text earned Vesalius an appointment as physician to the Holy Roman Emperor Charles V.

through hollow nerves. If you stick your finger in a fire, he believed, the heat sets off a "spirit" who dashes as fast as he can through the hollow tubes of the nerves to your brain to let it know to make your finger jerk back.

What is important is that Descartes sparked interest in how reflexes work. Perhaps his idea about

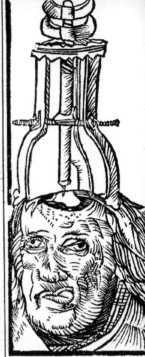

this process is not all that strange. Electrochemical impulses actually do race through the nervous system. The pain signal moves very quickly to the spinal cord and results in motor neurons causing a reflex action immediately, which makes you jerk back your finger.

These woodcuts depict the ancient practice of trepanning. Trephines were surgical instruments that cut circular pieces of bone. Trepanning is believed to be the oldest form of surgery in human history.

Then the signal continues on to inform the brain of what happened. The signal to the spinal cord and the return signal to jerk back are very fast. But so is the message that continues on to update the brain.

Descartes also promoted the idea of dualism, which says that the brain and the mind are two totally separate entities. He believed that the pineal body, a tiny organ in the center of the brain, was an exchange station where the spirits of the mind interacted with the physical brain. Dualism is rejected by modern science, although its influence has remained powerful over the centuries.

THE MODERN AGE

In the seventeenth century, brain science as we know it began. In 1667, English anatomist Thomas Willis (1621–1675) published a book called *Pathologiae cerebri et nervosi generis specimen,* which discussed the pathology and neurophysiology of the brain. Willis was the son of a farmer. At the time he entered Oxford University, he intended to have a career in the church, but then he changed his mind and focused on medicine. Willis would develop new theories about epilepsy and other convulsive diseases, and he would also provide early insights that were useful to psychiatry, the

medical study of mental disorders. The term "neurology" was first used in his book, which also contained dynamic illustrations of the nervous system by Christopher Wren, the famous architect who designed Saint Paul's Cathedral in London. Willis was an early believer in the idea that chemistry controlled human functions, including the brain. While most of his ideas were not quite correct, he pushed later scientists in the right direction.

The great English physician Thomas Willis was one of the first members of the Royal Society of London. He also wrote guides for staying well during the plague and for treating those infected.

In the eighteenth century, people began to think about how the brain is structured. A major figure here was Emanuel Swedenborg (1688–1772).

Emanuel Swedenborg made numerous discoveries, some of which have only been proven in the last 100 years. One of his findings was the respiratory movement of brain tissues.

Although he is remembered as a theologian and philosopher, he was also an important scientific thinker. His study of the brain and the nervous system included the first accurate understanding of how the cerebral cortex, the conscious thinking part of the brain, works.

One other early pioneer was Joseph Gall (1758–1828). He essentially did away with Descartes's idea of dualism and said that the mind is not a separate entity from the physical brain. He carried out anatomical studies of the brain that strongly suggested that mental processes come out of the physical

brain. He was also the first scientist to suggest that mental functions are localized; that is, specific parts of the brain carry out specific functions.

THE PHYSICAL BRAIN

The brain is an organ of the body, just like the heart, lungs, and kidneys. It is a physical lump of billions of cells, hollow spaces, and blood vessels. It burns oxygen, creates electricity, and exchanges chemical substances. It can be seen, touched, handled, and put in a glass jar, if it is cut out of the skull. On the average, it weighs about 3 pounds (1.4 kilograms). It takes a considerable amount of energy to fuel the brain. Although it makes up only 2 percent of average total body weight, it is responsible for almost 20 percent of the body's metabolic actions. It takes a lot of blood sugar, or glucose, to keep the brain functioning.

The brain is at the culmination of the nervous system that enters from the spinal cord through a hole

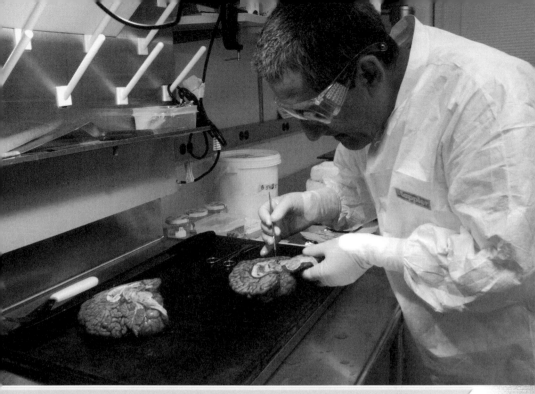

Donations of organs to science enable researchers to come closer to finding cures for disorders of the brain. A "normal" brain may be compared with that of a person who suffered from schizophrenia or Parkinson's disease during his or her lifetime.

in the bottom of the skull. The brain controls bodily mechanical functions such as the pumping of the heart and the breathing of the lungs. It also regulates temperature, blood pressure, and other functions. The brain receives and interprets the sensory information coming in from the eyes, ears, tongue, nose, and the skin. It

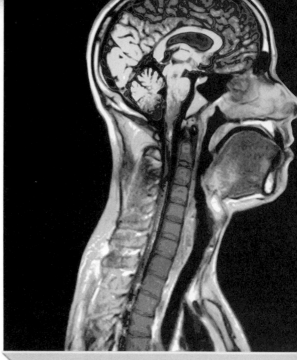

controls physical motion and balance. It is because of the brain that you are aware yourself. It lets you think, dream, have feelings, and make choices.

The brain and spinal cord are protected by the backbone and skull, as well as a fluid that acts as a shock absorber.

A lot of operations go on in your brain that you are not conscious of. You may think, for example, that to walk is a conscious choice. In order to walk, your brain must give specific commands: Lift the right leg about 4 to 6 inches (10 to 15 centimeters) off the ground, more if you are running. Swing that leg forward about 12 to 18 inches (30 to 46 cm) and at the instant it touches the ground shift your body weight forward onto that leg. Do this all at once in a smooth action. Now, lift the left leg and follow the same procedures. You don't have to think about such actions consciously most of the time.

The mind is the product of the brain. The mind is all your thoughts, memories, emotions, and perceptions of yourself and the world around you. The mind is the essence of who you are, but without the brain the mind cannot exist.

THE PARTS OF THE BRAIN

The brain didn't just pop into existence a few hundred centuries ago. It has evolved from the more primitive brains and nervous systems of other creatures. If we think of the brain in this way, we can identify its three major parts. The hindbrain is more or less at the back and bottom of the cranial cavity and was the first part to evolve. Basic body functions, such as regulation of the heart and lungs, are controlled from here. This is sometimes called the reptilian brain. The prehistoric animals that we evolved from needed this part of the brain just to stay alive, as we do. Next comes the midbrain. This serves as the control center for sensory functions. This is sometimes called the old mammalian brain. The third part of the brain is the forebrain, where our high-level thinking functions are controlled. This is sometimes called the new mammalian brain.

In brain evolution, species preserve the structures for basic function, such as the hindbrain depicted here, while acquiring more complex ones.

Let's break down the parts a bit further. The largest part of the brain is the cerebrum. The cerebrum is divided into two halves, called hemispheres, connected by a mass of nerve fibers called the corpus callosum. The two hemispheres control opposite sides of the body. Each hemisphere deals with different activities, but the two halves are well connected and work together. This idea of a "split brain" has fascinated neuroscientists for a long time, and many studies have tried to map out what each half does and how the two halves are coordinated. Roger Sperry (1913–1994) won the Nobel Prize in 1981 for his work in showing how each side of the brain functions and how the two parts work together to create a whole mind. If the two halves lose contact with each other, we still function, but in strange ways.

Each hemisphere is covered with a crinkled layer of material, about 0.25 inch (0.6 cm) thick, called the cerebral cortex. It is wrinkled and folded to increase its surface area in order to give more room for processing information. If it were flattened and the wrinkles ironed out, it would be about 300 to 400 square inches (1,935 to 2,581 sq cm) in area. Having the wrinkles is like adding many gigabytes to your computer.

Other areas of the brain perform specific functions. The frontal lobes control planning and decision making and override our more primitive behaviors.

These lobes are right behind your forehead. Just behind your frontal lobes is the motor cortex, which helps control intentional movements. The parietal lobes lie behind the first two lobes. These are concerned with perception of stimuli related to touch, pressure, temperature, and pain. The occipital lobes are located at the back of the brain, behind the parietal lobes and the temporal lobes. They are involved with vision. The temporal lobes are on the side of the brain close to the temples. They are related to hearing, memory, and emotions. The hypothalamus is about the size of a pea, but it does an incredible amount of work in controlling the various automatic functions of the body. Here is where your temperature is regulated and where you feel hunger and thirst. It also helps regulate hormones. The amygdala is an almond-shaped structure that is involved in memory functions. The hippocampus is related to emotion, conditioning, and memory storage. If your hippocampus quits working, you won't remember new information for more than a minute or two.

BRAIN STEM

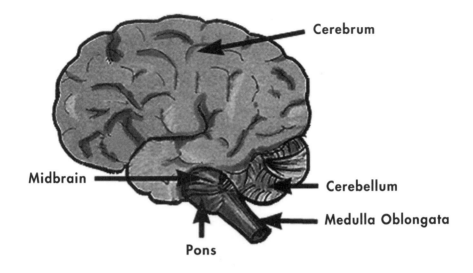

The midbrain carries sensory information. Its parts include the cerebellum, which controls voluntary movement and balance; the medulla oblongata, which is dedicated to basic body functions; the pons, which serves as a bridge between the cerebellum and medulla; and the cerebrum, which is responsible for higher cognitive functions.

The thalamus is involved in motor control and the relaying of sensory signals. The pituitary gland, again a small structure, uses hormones to monitor and control other endocrine glands in the body. The limbic system is a network of some of the other parts of the brain (amygdala, pituitary gland, thalamus) that are related

to your emotions and to memory storage. Emotions are closely related to what we remember.

We have traveled a long way since the days when people believed that nerves were hollow tubes with spirits running through them and that ghosts dwelt in the cavities of our brain and fought over what is right and wrong. Scientists began to rely on observations and experimentation to find the truth. In order to do their work, new technologies and new methods of investigation had to be developed. In the following chapters, we will turn our attention to some of the people who developed and cleverly used these technologies to discover what the brain/mind is and how it works.

2

About Neuroscience

Understanding the brain and the mind requires the input of both biology and chemistry. It also needs physics and mathematical models. The viewpoints of psychologists and the skills of technicians who work with computers, microscopes, imaging machines, and other devices also come into play. In this chapter and the next

two chapters, we will look at three major fields of study devoted to the brain and the mind: neuroscience, psychology, and cognitive science. By looking at the scientific discoveries made in these three areas, we can paint a good picture of what we know about the mind. Let's look first at neuroscience. Neuroscience views the functions of the brain and the mind as the result of what brain cells do.

NEURONS

The brain could not be understood until we knew what brain cells are. The first major step in this direction occurred in 1839 when German cytologist Theodor Schwann (1810–1882) proposed that the nerve system is made up of individual nervous cells. Soon after this, it was discovered that nerve cells are not exactly like other body cells. Nerve cells are called neurons, a term coined by Wilhelm Waldeyer (1836–1921) in 1891. These neurons control consciousness, memory, sensation, and all

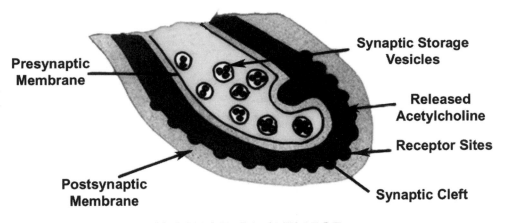

Presynaptic Membrane

Synaptic Storage Vesicles

Released Acetylcholine

Receptor Sites

Postsynaptic Membrane

Synaptic Cleft

CLOSE UP OF SYNAPSE

An impulse triggers synaptic storage vesicles to release the neurotransmitter (acetyl choline) that begins to make its way to the neighboring neuron. Once inside the synaptic cleft, it binds with proteins that will enable this action.

other bodily functions. You have approximately 100 billion of them in your head.

Neurons have three major parts. The cell body contains the nucleus, like all cells. Nerve cells have short receptor extensions called dendrites. There are many of these on a single neuron. Nerve cells also

have a longer extension called an axon. The axon coming out of the neuron connects to other neurons, both locally and to cells in other regions of the body. There can be many such connections from this single axon. Otto Friedrich Karl Deiters (1834–1863) first postulated that neurons have dendrites and axons. The dendrites are the primary receiving stations for information from other cells, and the axons send signals to other cells.

Neurons have many of the basic characteristics of all body cells but with one important difference: neurons process information. Billions of microscopic neurons, when operating together, store and process information. These interactions account for what you think, feel, and do. They create your mind. Mental events, such as memory and learning, are the result of changes in the connections between neurons. When you have new experiences and sensations, new neural connections are established and your brain changes. The brain you had sixty seconds ago is not the same brain you have right now. Think about that.

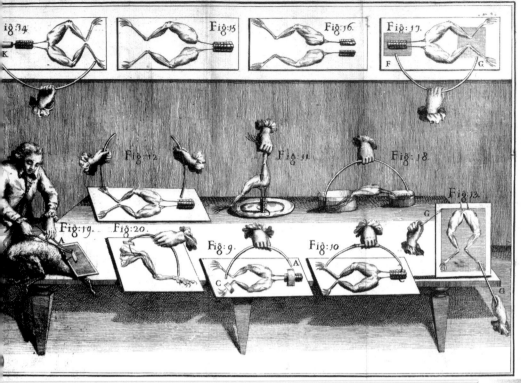

Here, Luigi Galvani is shown experimenting on the effects of electricity on frog's legs. Alessandro Volta challenged Galvani, saying that only the two metals were generating charges, aided by the moist environment of the muscle, but Galvani then generated a charge by touching one frog's nerve with that of another.

How do neurons do this? They do it by encoding information in neural patterns. A particular memory, for example, is not stored in one nerve cell but in a grid of nerve cells connected by their axons and dendrites. When that particular grid of neurons becomes electrically and chemically active, the mind recalls that memory. Early on, scientists suspected that something

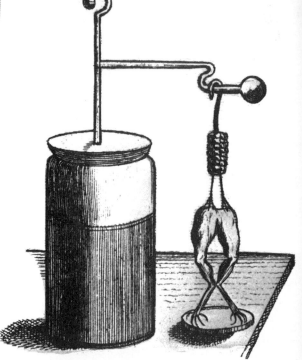

electrical happens in the brain. Italian scientists Luigi Galvani (1737–1798) and Alessandro Volta (1745–1827) both believed that such a thing as "animal electricity" existed. An eel or an electric ray can generate an electrical current that will make the hairs on your head stand straight up.

Galvani also connected frog legs to a Leyden jar. He concluded that charged fluid ran through the nervous system, activating muscles.

Sometime around 1780, Galvani discovered that he could make the muscles in the legs of a frog jump by stimulating them with a rotating static electrical generator or with a Leyden jar, an early version of an electrical storage battery. What he actually set out to do was to show that lightning was an electrical spark. During an electrical storm, he hung up some frog legs on a metal railing on the balcony of his house, with brass hooks in the muscles. The muscles jumped, but they also jumped when there wasn't lightning. Muscle contractions occurred when the tissues were in contact with two different metals. It had nothing to do with external electricity. Galvani concluded that electricity was coming from the legs of his frogs. He decided that "animal electricity" was causing this phenomenon. Clearly, internal tissues in an organism can produce electricity. Galvani's discoveries led to the term "galvanize," which means to stimulate with an electric current. His experiments would later inspire novelist Mary Shelley in writing *Frankenstein*, published in 1878.

Galvani's experiments began the fundamental studies of neurophysiology and neurology. Later, Emil Heinrich Du Bois-Reymond (1818–1896) developed a sensitive device that could detect electricity in a frog's leg. Hermann von Helmholtz (1821–1894) measured the speed of frog nerve impulses and determined them to be about 88.6 feet (27 m) per second. Frogs have made a major contribution to neuroscience!

A landmark event in neuroscience occurred when German neuropsychiatrist Hans Berger (1873–1941) discovered that the continuous electrical activity of the brain could be recorded. He is known as the father of electroencephalography. The electroencephalograph (EEG) can measure the weak electrical signals of the brain. Metal disks are stuck to the scalp of the patient, and the signals picked up are multiplied thousands of times, recorded with a galvanometer, and drawn on charting paper. Nowadays, computers translate the wave inputs into numbers and display them on a screen or print them out in some meaningful format.

By the end of the nineteenth century, scientists believed that neurons were electrically connected in some way. This was called the reticular theory. This theory visualized the nervous system as an elaborate network with all the neurons wired together, preset to carry out the brain's functions. But not all scientists accepted the reticular theory, and for many decades they debated whether neurons were actually physically wired together or if they communicated some other way. Finally, it was shown that the neurons were not physically connected, but that the axons and dendrites of individual nerve cells were separated by tiny gaps where chemical interactions moved signals from one cell to another.

The primary reason that scientists couldn't agree on how neurons communicate with each other was that the techniques for studying cells were still not sensitive enough. The microscopes of the day just didn't have the power to show matter this small. The situation improved when Italian physiologist Camillo Golgi (1843–1926) developed a special staining method for highlighting the structures of nerve cells and nerve fibers. His stain used potassium dichromate saturated with silver nitrate. When he applied the chemical compound to nerve tissue, a few of the cells would absorb it and transport it to all of the tissue's branches, and this made the cells prominent under the microscope. The cells stood out vividly with shades of gold, brown, and black, giving scientists detailed information about their structure.

One of the greatest neuroscientists in the world, Santiago Ramón y Cajal (1852–1934) of Spain,

Santiago Ramón y Cajal studied medicine, made discoveries about the nervous system, and applied his drawing talents to anatomy atlases.

improved on Golgi's staining method by using silver dichromate. Cajal's technique was more sensitive and showed nerve tissue in even more detail. He was able to describe almost all of the details of the nervous system. His observations revealed that networks of neurons are not continuous. There are tiny gaps between the cells.

Cajal's work led scientists to believe that we have trillions of gaps in our brains between our neurons and that these tiny gaps are fundamental to the communication between neurons. A single neuron can send information to many other cells at the same time, creating the appropriate connections to trigger the proper memory, sensation, or motor action. The connections are continuously changing at every instant, reflecting a highly dynamic system. These patterns of connections represent the information the brain is processing. This is the neuron theory of how the brain works.

Ironically, in 1906 Cajal shared the Nobel Prize with Golgi, although Golgi believed in the reticular theory and Cajal believed in the neuron theory. In the end, both were right. There are trillions of gaps, but there are some direct hookups as well. The transmitting end of an axon, the dendrite receptor, and the gap between them are collectively known as a synapse. Sir Charles Sherrington (1857–1952) coined the term in 1897. The tiny gaps, called the synaptic clefs, are about 20 to 30 nanometers across. A nanometer is a millionth of a millimeter. After Cajal's work became

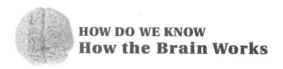
known, the next problem was to determine just how information gets across the gap between neurons.

To answer the question of how neurons carry messages across the gaps, we turn again to frogs. German pharmacologist Otto Loewi (1873–1961) examined two frog hearts, one with the vagus nerve still attached and one without the nerve. The vagus nerve is a major nerve that runs from the head to the abdomen. He put each beating heart in a jar of saltwater that more or less resembled regular body fluid. He shot a little charge of electricity into the heart in the first jar. This changed the rate of the heartbeat. Then he took some of the liquid from the first jar and injected it into the heart in the second jar. The second heart changed its rate of beating just like the first heart! Some chemical had been released into the solution in the first jar, and that chemical had affected the heart in the second jar. Thus it was clear that neurons send information across the synaptic gap with chemicals. These chemicals were later named neurotransmitters.

The signal coming across the gap is not a steady flow, like a water faucet that has been turned on. An electrical impulse builds up at the end of the axon. When a certain threshold is reached, as if the neuron needs to measure the importance of the signal before triggering the transfer of information, the axon releases molecules of the neurotransmitter. Neurons are electrically charged. They contain ions, atoms, or molecules with an imbalance of electrons, so that at any instant they might have a net positive or negative charge. This creates an electrical potential, a force between the inside and outside of the neuron's membrane. When a neuron is excited, ions flow through dilated passages in the axon's membranes and alter the voltage, or the force of electrical attraction. This charge of electricity is called an action potential, and it moves swiftly down the axon.

When the critical threshold is reached, the neuron "fires off" across the gap. But this firing is not electrical. What happens is a small vesicle or cavity of

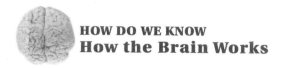
neurotransmitters at the end of the axon opens and releases its contents. When the vesicle breaks open, the neurotransmitters dash into the synaptic gap and rapidly attach themselves to the receiving dendrites on the other side of the gap. This is not haphazard. The neurotransmitters can fit only into certain places, like keys in a lock. They quickly find their proper place and attach.

How does the brain keep all of these messages balanced without going haywire? It does this by having two types of neurotransmitters, excitatory and inhibitory. The excitatory chemicals tell the next neuron to fire in the same way and pass the signal along. The inhibitory chemicals tell the next neuron not to fire. In this way the communication system is kept under control and the information gets processed properly. It is now known that with a disease like epilepsy, which causes uncontrollable muscle spasms, not enough inhibitory neurotransmitters are generated, and nerve cells are firing off haphazardly and uncontrollably.

Australian physiologist Sir John Eccles is pictured here in 1961 at the University of Canberra. His research into the types of synapses between motor nerves and skeletal muscle was of later use in implementing paralyzing drugs for anesthesia.

Sir John Eccles (1903–1997) was one of the scientists who gave us an understanding of how synapses work by using electroencephalography. Eccles was a Rhodes scholar who had concentrated in natural sciences. He then became a research fellow under the famous neuroscientist Sir Charles Sherrington. In 1963, he received the Nobel Prize for showing that both electrical and chemical processes were involved in synapses.

MAPPING THE BRAIN

In the nineteenth century, scientists began to demonstrate that specific mental processes are related to specific areas of the brain. They began, literally, to map the brain. The idea that different parts of the brain are responsible for different functions goes as least as far back as Franz Gall (1758–1828), famous for the founding of phrenology, the "science" of determining brain functions or personality by feeling the lumps on the skull. Although we now know that this is ludicrous, Gall did raise the question of whether brain functions were located in specific parts of the brain. This encouraged other scientists to seriously explore the idea.

Animals were first used for brain mapping studies. Pierre Flourens (1794–1867) used rabbits and pigeons to show that different parts of the brain are responsible for different functions. When he surgically removed certain parts of the brain, certain functions in the animal stopped. Sometimes he went too far. The animals

Franz Joseph Gall discovered that cell bodies make up the brain's gray matter and that the white matter contained fibers.

shut down their mental activity and died when he tampered with their brain stems. These studies showed that specific parts of the brain control breathing, circulation, and movement and that the higher levels of mental processing (conscious thought) occur in the cerebral hemispheres.

Soon after Flourens's work, scientists began to pay attention to the locations in human brains where particular functions were centered. For example, the part of the brain related to speech was first identified in 1836 when Marc Dax (1770–1837), a French doctor, reported that he had noticed that some patients lost the power to speak when they suffered damage to the left side of the

43

brain. Paul Broca (1824–1880), also from France, entered medical school at the age of seventeen and graduated three years later. He took neuroscience a step further in 1864 by declaring that he knew for sure that people speak with the left side of their brains. He gathered data by doing autopsies on people who had lost the power to speak before they died. His most famous patient was called Tan. That wasn't his real name, but the medical staff at the hospital called him that because the only thing he could say was "Tan! Tan! Tan!" Broca identified a particular place in the left side of Tan's brain, a little bit forward of the midsection, that was damaged. This place is now known as Broca's area. A few years later, Carl Wernicke (1848–1904) identified another area of the brain that, when damaged, did not inhibit speech but made everything said nonsensical. People with this problem also had trouble understanding speech when someone talked to them. This part of the brain is now known as Wernicke's area.

In 1981, David Hubel (1926–) and Torsten Wiesel (1924–) showed how the retina in the eye coordinates with the visual cortex to help you see. The visual cortex lies at the back of the skull, so signals from the optic nerve have to go all the way to the back of the brain, where a network of neurons records the relationship between objects as if displayed on an inner picture screen. Representation of visual images is localized in this rear area of the brain.

The regions of the brain that control motor action, located in the cerebral cortex, have also been mapped in great detail. For example, we know that if one part of the left hemisphere of the cerebral cortex is stimulated with electricity, the person's right foot will suddenly kick out. Stimulating another part of the cortex makes the hand jerk. By the way, only a small part of the motor cortex is devoted to control of the legs. A much larger portion of the cortex controls the hands and face. In terms of human evolution, hand movements and facial expressions were much more important to our physical and social development, and so more nerve cells were dedicated to controlling these parts of the body.

The mapping of the brain is a continuing research activity and is accelerating with the development of new technology. Neuroscientists have given us insight into how the brain is organized and how it works on the electrochemical level. But there is more to the story. The next step is to think about how the mind creates the self that makes us unique. For this, we turn to psychology.

3

Theories in Psychology

Psychology has been called the science of the mind. Neurons, synapses, and electrochemical actions make up the physical nuts and bolts of the brain. Psychology interprets the mind that those nuts and bolts produce. Psychology attempts to find out why people do what they do. Psychologists don't deny that electrochemical

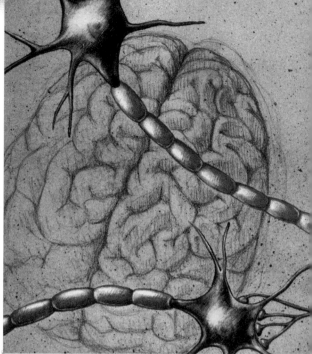

reactions are basic to what the brain does. Instead, they search for the causes that drive these activities. The brain is full of motives, memories, and emotions, and there are sensory signals coming in from the environment outside the brain that con-

Human emotions may be processed in individual brain cells in the right prefrontal cortex. There, neurons (shown above) categorize visual emotional information.

stantly alter the mind. Psychologists see the brain as a machine, a kind of automobile with many complicated working parts. But what steers the automobile in a particular direction or brings it to a stop? Sometimes a breakdown on the neuronal level causes the machine to work in a peculiar way, but most of our behavior seems to be determined at a higher level, the level of the mind.

Psychologists believe that past experience is fundamental to understanding present behavior and that future behavior is encouraged or inhibited by what we experience with our environment. That is to say, psychologists believe that to a greater or lesser extent behavior is learned rather than "hardwired" into the network of nerve cells in the brain. Of course, there is a great deal of debate over how much we learn as opposed to how much behavior is instinctual, and many mental illnesses once thought to be the result of mental conditioning of some kind are now known to have physical causes. Nevertheless, the basis of psychology is the study of the thoughts and thought processes of human beings rather than the underlying electrical or biochemical processes of the brain.

Psychology had its beginnings in philosophy. As modern science developed and we began to understand the physical brain, philosophical questions about the mind turned into scientific questions and

psychology slowly began to evolve into a science. Early experimental psychology was based on a technique called self-introspection, which looks at internal mental events as something we can observe, measure, and explain. Wilhelm Wundt (1832–1920) pioneered this idea, beginning with the processes that occur when something stimulates the sense organs. Why do you jump when you hear a sudden loud noise or jerk back your hand when you touch something hot? And what did you think about when these actions took place?

Wundt moved on to the study of conscious experiences, and he developed protocols for self-examination of the mind. If I ask you to squeeze a rubber ball, what can you tell me about the experience? Wundt collected such introspective data and used it in attempts to discover how the mind works. In 1879, he established the first laboratory in the world dedicated to experimental psychology at Leipzig, Germany. Over the years, many of the world's future psychologists

William James believed that the self was embodied and free will established an independent human being.

studied there. For several decades, up until the 1920s, psychologists used Wundt's methods. Experimental techniques for studying the mind have changed, but Wundt is applauded for showing us that psychology can utilize experimental methods.

William James (1842–1910) tried to bridge the gaps between philosophy, physiology, and psychology. In his classic book, *The Principles of Psychology* (1890), he discusses ideas that are basic to psychology: how brains function, what is perception, what is memory, and so on. James was following Wundt's technique of introspection, which was popular at that time.

SIGMUND FREUD

Sigmund Freud (1856–1939) is the most famous psychologist who ever lived. Born in the Austro-Hungarian Empire, Freud lived in Vienna from the time he was four years old until it was occupied by Germany in 1938. He then moved to London to escape persecution for being of Jewish descent. Words related to him are common in our vocabulary, such as the term "Freudian slip," which means saying something you didn't intend to say because it was generated by your subconscious mind. Freud made profound contributions to the field of psychology, although some of his ideas are still controversial.

Freud is best remembered for his ideas about the importance of unconscious processes that help to drive the mind. He believed that when we grow out of childhood we push frightening or confusing feelings and ideas deep down into our subconscious mind and that these conflicts come out and affect our behavior when we grow up. As adults, we suppress or push out of our

Sigmund Freud's idea of the unconscious mind was in direct opposition to the dominant belief of the day that people could learn about themselves and their world, and implement rational control over both. Freud considered this to be delusional, suggesting instead that people are governed by thoughts and instincts that exist "below the surface."

consciousness any thoughts that are regarded as unpleasant by adult society, such as sexual desires. Freud's most famous idea was his tripartite (three-part) model of our mental processes. The id is the part of the mind that deals with basic instincts, such as sexual desires. The superego is the part of the mind that continually reminds us of what is acceptable social behavior. The ego is the conscious self that results from the conflicts and interactions between the id and the superego

and that charts for us a course of practical action between basic instincts and acceptable ethical behavior. Freud did not intend for the id, the ego, and the superego to be thought of as having specific locations in the brain. Instead they were meant to be a framework that the mind used to evaluate the acceptability of its actions.

Freud also developed a therapeutic technique for probing into these conflicts between id and superego, which he called psychoanalysis. In a controlled setting, the psychoanalyst questions the patient, who talks out his or her problem. The psychoanalyst listens carefully to the patient and, with enough experience, is able to recognize certain words, expressions, ideas, and even recalled dreams as symbols of underlying problems. Freud believed that the superego would censor the real expression of unacceptable feelings and disguise those feelings with symbols. It is the job of the psychoanalyst to discover the meaning of the symbols as the patient talks out the problem. Once the underlying problem— guilt or anger toward a parent, for example—is recognized by the patient, it can be dealt with.

Psychoanalysis is an attempt at self-understanding. The analyst tries to lead the patient toward recognition of the source of his or her discomfort, and the patient is cured simply by understanding how a deep childhood fear or anxiety has intertwined itself with some aspect of daily life and been given a significance that is abnormal. Psychoanalysis is controversial because, first of all, the process of working with an analyst can take many years, and rates and degrees of cure are not well documented. Furthermore, modern neuroscience has found simpler explanations in biochemistry and faster and more effective cures for many mental illnesses through the use of drugs.

BEHAVIORISM

In the first half of the twentieth century, psychology took a sharp turn away from introspection toward a school of psychological thought known as behaviorism. The idea behind behaviorism is that the psychologist can know all about the patient by observing his or her

behavior rather than by searching for deep, underlying mechanisms. We behave the way we do because our previous behavior was reinforced by a positive stimulus. If there is no positive stimulus, a person will sooner or later abandon a particular behavior.

An early pioneer in this area was the Russian physiologist Ivan Pavlov (1849–1936). It had been his parents' wish that Pavlov would become a priest; however, after reading the works of Charles Darwin, Pavlov set his sights on chemistry and psychology. Pavlov would put forward the idea of the conditioned reflex. If a certain behavior results in a positive or desirable outcome, then that behavior produces a favored neural pathway in the brain and the behavior becomes almost like a reflex, that is, an automatic response. The classic example from Pavlov's experiments is that of the dog who hears a bell every time he is fed. After a very short time, the dog will salivate whenever he hears the bell, whether or not food is served. A new neural connection has been established between the bell and the act of salivating. Pavlov believed that most human behavior in all its complexity

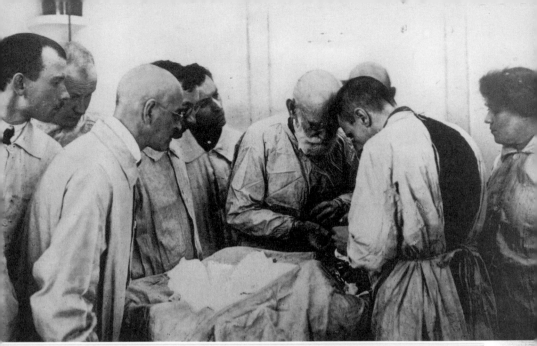

Between the years of 1891 and 1900 Ivan Pavlov (center) did a series of experiments on dogs using a surgical technique that allowed him to observe bodily processes as they took place. His discovery of the nervous system's major role in digestion led him to the study of conditioned reflexes.

is built up from simple or more complicated sets of conditioned reflexes. Pavlov was trying to measure behavior objectively without the need for internal mental mechanisms like ids or superegos, and so he is considered an early adherent of behaviorism.

There were several major players in the behaviorism movement. The American psychologist John Watson (1878–1958) was an early advocate of the theory. He stated that self-introspection is subjective and that

behaviorism, on the other hand, is objective. He studied different animals and tried to find universal laws of behavior that could be applied to humans. He began to study the behavior of children, believing that at this early stage humans could be seen to be merely more complicated versions of lower animals. To Watson, it was very simple. If you want to understand people, just study what they do. He didn't think that you could depend on what people tell you about themselves, which was the classic technique of psychoanalysis.

B. F. Skinner (1904–1990) is probably the name that we most often associate with behaviorism. Originally from Pennsylvania, Skinner moved to New York City in the 1920s to pursue a career as a writer. He changed his mind and then enrolled in Harvard to study psychology. He took behaviorism a step beyond Pavlov by showing that we can condition humans to do things the way we want them to. He devised ways to reward animals if they performed a command, like pulling a certain lever for a pellet of food, and to punish animals if they failed. For example, if a rat hit the wrong lever, it would get a little electrical shock. This system of reward and punishment led to the idea of behavior modification. Skinner's system was based on the idea of operant conditioning. A person—through his or her actions—"operates" on the environment and receives either a reinforcing stimulus, a negative stimulus, or no stimulus at all. Behavior is reinforced or rendered "extinct" by the type and frequency of the stimulus. Behaviorists were empiricists; that is, they solely relied on results of objectively observed data in an attempt to explain human actions. The methods of behaviorism were not unscientific, but they were unsatisfactory to those investigators who felt the need for a theory of the underlying mental mechanisms. By studying the types of stimuli a person was exposed to, a behaviorist could predict behavior, but he or she could not explain it.

It is obvious that we develop psychologically over our entire lifetimes, not just as we are growing up. But our minds do develop in special ways in our early years. The Swiss psychologist and philosopher Jean Piaget (1896–1980) spent many years of his life studying mental

development in young people. He proposed that we have significant milestones in our development. Between birth and about two years of age, we develop basic motor skills. From the age of three to six or seven years, we begin to have mental representation. We begin to think of the world as something outside ourselves and separate from who we are. By the age of twelve or so, we have developed the ability to manipulate symbols logically. After the age of twelve, we learn to think hypothetically in order to solve problems.

Piaget's theory of this progression of the development of the mind is debatable, but his basic ideas do make us realize that our minds progress and develop from the moment we are born until the moment we die. Change is the most persistent condition of the mind.

SOME REMAINING PUZZLES

There are fundamental aspects of the mind that still puzzle us, although we do have some understanding and a lot of opinions. Intelligence is a concept that we

Jean Piaget believed that by correcting a child when their theories of how things work are wrong inhibits the child from rethinking the idea and developing important learning skills.

think we understand, and yet it is one that eludes us when we try to define it scientifically. Is it the ability to reason? Is it the size of our vocabulary and how fast we think? Is it how much we remember? Or is it the ability to compose music or solve mathematical problems? Perhaps it is all of these. *Webster's New Collegiate Dictionary* defines "intelligence" as "the ability to learn or understand or to deal with new or trying situations" and "the ability to apply knowledge to manipulate one's environment or to think abstractly." A more scientific definition might be that intelligence is the measure of how well the brain processes information. Is there any biological basis for

what we call intelligence, or is it just a skill that some people exhibit under certain circumstances, while others exhibit it under other circumstances? In other words, is the chess player as intelligent as the novelist, and are their two skills related to the same mental process?

Memory is another imperfectly understood phenomenon. Without memory, we could not experience life in quite the same way. Memory allows us to jump back in time and reconstruct where we came from. It provides an instant-by-instant continuity to our existence and therefore creates the sense of self. But it is not perfect. At best it produces an incomplete image of what happened, and it is often not very accurate. It is a summary of reality that is supported by beliefs and prejudices about what usually is supposed to happen in certain situations. We remember in terms of what we believe to be true about our world, and our memories may fool us.

Learning and memory are intertwined. There is no such thing as learning without memory. Scientists believe that both are physically explained by synaptic connections. For example, as you improve your chess game, synaptic connections are reconfiguring in your brain. Learning is the result of the brain restructuring the connections of the neurons. Neurons begin to respond more strongly to signals they have received many times before, deepening the connection between a certain stimulus, like an opponent's chess move, and the new, learned response.

Emotion is also tied to memory. All of us experience emotion—anger, love, fear, joy, sadness, courage, surprise, grief, despair, and passion. Memories associated with strong emotions are more easily called to mind. Emotion is closely related to physiological changes in the body. For example, when we are very sad, tears come to our eyes. When we get angry, we turn red in the face and may clench our fists. When we are excited, we breathe more rapidly and adrenaline flows, giving us heightened awareness. Emotion is a state that your mind brings about spontaneously, rather than by deliberate conscious thought.

At one time, scientists thought that the mind used specific parts of the brain to evoke emotion, but

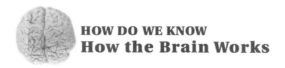

now we know that many parts of the brain are involved. The limbic system is centrally involved, which makes sense because it is also involved with memory. Because emotions are so interconnected to the body's physiological state, they can be related to health in very powerful ways. Doctors urge people to avoid emotional stress precisely because too much of it can cause physical damage to the body.

Neuroscientists have demonstrated that electrical stimulation in the temporal lobes of the brain can produce subjective emotional experiences, but that doesn't quite explain how the electric stimulation generates all the shades and ranges of emotions that we have. Research is expanding in this area as scientists have come to realize that emotion is a fundamental function of the mind.

Modern psychology accepts the fact that the electrochemical mechanisms in the physical brain are basic to creating the mind. But psychology tries to give us insight into who we are as beings who have grown up in

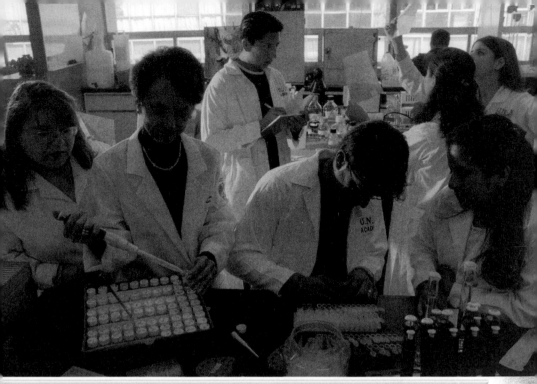

Professor of Neuroscience Ana Maria Lopez-Colomer (second from left) has done award-winning research on how diseases of the retina can lead to total sight loss. Here, she leads a group of students through an experiment at the Universidad Autonoma de Mexico. Neuroscientific research leads to a better understanding of the brain.

the real world and who must respond to it effectively, regardless of how our nerve tissues are organized inside the brain. It is the field of cognitive science, however, that studies how the brain actually processes information, and we turn to this in the next chapter.

4

The World of Cognitive Science

Cognition is defined as the act of becoming acquainted with, or knowing, including both awareness and judgment. Cognitive science deals with the structures and processes inside our brain that enable us to become aware by performing billions of computations across the neuronal network.

Cognitive science combines methods from neuroscience, psychology, computer science, linguistics, and other areas to study cognition in human beings. In a sense, cognitive science was a revolt against behaviorism, because it insisted that mental events could not be understood without looking inside the brain. The new cognitive scientists said that it was not enough just to observe how people were behaving. We needed to explain why and how behavior was initiated inside the mind of an organism.

THE COMPUTATIONAL MIND

Cognitive scientists view the mind as an information storage and retrieval system, much like the modern computer. The brain does its work of processing, storing, retrieving, and computing bits of information. Awareness, visual interpretation, language, planning, and other mental processes, both conscious and unconscious, are the results of this computation. The analogy of the computer to describe the brain is useful in understanding the differences as well as the similarities. Computers and brains both use electricity to function, but brains also rely heavily on chemical reactions, whereas

An MRI scan can take up to one hour to complete, with each set of images taking two to fifteen minutes to be performed.

computers don't. Though they may appear to be more sophisticated, most computers can actually perform only one task at a time, very rapidly of course, but they execute only one instruction at a time. Brains appear to work in a non-linear fashion, more through free association than working their way through sets of instructions. Brains are aware of what they are doing.

Computers are not. Both can learn from experience, but computers never forget anything you tell them, while the brain often forgets.

Computers are a major tool for cognitive scientists in many ways. Computers are used when we need to process large amounts of data. As the brain does its work, it produces a cascade of data, and when we are conducting neurophysiological experiments, we need computers to keep up with this. For example, computers can convert the electrical impulses from sensors attached to the skull or from modern imaging machines into digital form. In digital form, this information can be converted into three-dimensional images of the brain that show increased activity in particular areas. This helps us to determine which regions of the brain are involved in different kinds of thinking. It can also help us to locate tumors or damaged blood vessels or areas of the brain that are not functioning properly.

Cognitive scientists can also use computers to study how the brain processes information. One way to

do this is to try to write computer programs to simulate the brain's thinking. In other words, we study the brain by pretending that the computer is a brain. Computer programs try to represent the characteristics of the real biological brain. The brain's information is stored in many different locations, and many calculations are going on at the same time, not just one by one, step by step, as with a computer. The complex network of inter-connected axons and dendrites in the brain creates many new and ever-changing pathways for new thought associations. This is a far more complex and flexible system than any computer program. Modern computers can perform parallel processing also but at nowhere near the level of complexity of the brain. The brain, furthermore, is influenced by its emotional state as it thinks. And it can recall memories in original ways that affect its decisions.

The brain moves information through a network of billions of neurons that are computing by firing off neurotransmitters in thousandths of a second. The

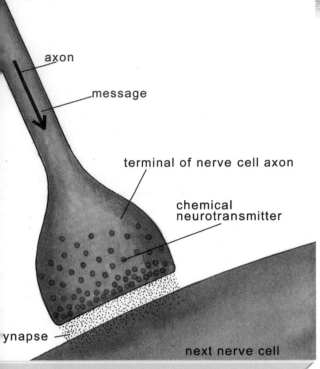

axon

message

terminal of nerve cell axon

chemical
neurotransmitter

synapse

next nerve cell

The released neurotransmitter can be diffused in the synaptic cleft by enzymatic breakdown or be absorbed back into the axon terminal.

information transmitted comes in the form of an action potential, an electric charge that moves down the cell's axon and triggers the release of a chemical at some of the nerve endings. Some chemicals pass the signal along to another neuron. Other chemicals inhibit the transmission of the signal. With each nerve cell having connections to dozens or even hundreds of other nerve cells, some receiving the new signals and some blocked from receiving them, it is a daunting task to imagine how the brain encodes its messages or how it decides which neurons will fire. In the old Morse code used for radio communications, the

information pattern lay in the number and sequence of dots and dashes transmitted. With the brain, the information lies in the number, the frequency, and the particular combination of firing spikes of a group of nerve cells. Information is encoded within the patterns of firings. This almost requires a new, three-dimensional view of how information can be stored, and we are a long way from understanding how it is done.

And when we do understand how the brain encodes information, we may still be a long way from understanding ourselves. For the brain is not the mind. A collection of electrochemically active nerve cells is not the same as the image in our memory of a person's face or the voice we hear inside our heads when we recall something someone said to us. We may eventually know everything there is to know about the switching and transmission system inside the brain, and we may still not be able to define such notions as consciousness or self-awareness.

ARTIFICIAL INTELLIGENCE

Whether we can ever understand human thought using computers, research is producing some very interesting experiments in the simulation of human thought or particular aspects of it. This field is known as artificial intelligence, or AI. We still hope to make computers act like brains, but we don't fully understand the mind and we don't know a lot about what intelligence really is. Our brains perform tasks so easily that we are surprised at the difficulties we have trying to program computers to do the same.

But there are many practical applications for computers that use a simplified low level of artificial intelligence. Robots of all kinds are used in the industrial world to control everything from welding torches to lasers. Medical diagnostic systems based on artificial intelligence are proving useful to busy health care workers. Computers can be set to fly airplanes, making course corrections and monitoring

fuel consumption. Computer programs have been designed that can play chess and even outperform human players. All of these systems must be capable of making decisions and analyzing the outcome of those decisions through feedback mechanisms, correcting choices that led to undesirable outcomes, and learning from experience.

If we have not yet duplicated the functions of the brain, this research has given us useful insight into how the brain processes information and just how complicated a process it is. We cannot make computers act like brains unless we understand how brains work in the first place. And trying to duplicate in the laboratory millions of years of evolutionary development is proving very difficult. The Honda Motor Company, for example, has built a new robot known as ASIMO (Advanced Step in Innovative Mobility) that can duplicate the natural walking motion of human beings. ASIMO can walk forward and backward, can turn corners, and can even climb up and down stairs.

The Honda Motor Company created the robot ASIMO for the purpose of one day being able to help people in need. ASIMO is 4 feet (1.2 m) tall and weighs 115 pounds (52 kg).

But just getting it to perform these simple mechanical tasks required enormous effort. Compared, say, to the quick movements and feints, the shifts of balance and reversals of direction, that a human basketball player makes as he or she moves down the court, ASIMO's ability to walk seems hopelessly primitive.

PIONEERS

The field of cognitive science has only emerged within the last fifty years. Many of its pioneers were initially

identified with other disciplines, such as artificial intelligence, neuroscience, and psychology, as there wasn't any such field of study until the 1950s.

In 1967, American scientist Allen Newell (1927–1992) designed a computer system called MERLIN. MERLIN was to be a tool to help construct artificial intelligence programs. Newell attempted to teach his computer problem-solving techniques and how to draw analogies by matching sets of data. It turned out to be a formidable undertaking, and Newell regarded MERLIN as a failure. But MERLIN is not seen as a failure by practitioners in the field of artificial intelligence. Instead, they see it as a reminder that the complexity of the human mind is not well understood and, therefore, does not reveal which way to proceed in trying to give computers intelligence. Newell earned an international reputation as one of the founders of artificial intelligence. He is also known for his work in the theory of human cognition and the development of computer software and hardware systems for complex information processing.

Marvin Minsky (1927–) received degrees in mathematics from both Harvard and Princeton. He built the first randomly wired neural network-learning machine, called SNARC (Stochastic Neural-Analog Reinforcement Computer), based on replicating mathematically what happens when synaptic transmissions occur in the brain. Minsky's computer would learn to favor certain switching patterns if they were triggered more frequently, in the same way that the mind stores memories and responses to common situations. It would build its own program as it worked, attempting to duplicate the human learning process. In the 1970s, Minsky and Seymour Papert, another revered mathematician, developed a theory called the society of the mind, which said that human intelligence is not the result of a few basic reasoning principles or mechanisms, but is the result of a vast number of interacting mechanisms, each evolved to handle a different task, but interacting to create a flexible brain that can handle all sorts of new problems.

Minsky also argued strongly for a simple and clear idea describing the relationship of the brain and the mind. The idea of a mind as something separate from a brain was contrary to the way Minsky understood nature. It led to all sorts of unanswerable questions, such as how the mind could work if it is not of the physical world. Is the mind like some sort of ghost inside the skull? Minsky took the view that whatever consciousness and self-awareness were, they were constructs based on the sensations created by the brain and its neural network.

John McCarthy (1927–) is another pioneer in the field of artificial intelligence who worked hard to apply formal mathematical logic to the common-sense reasoning processes that human beings actually use. Common sense is important because it answers questions that are not specifically asked and yet are critical to the solution of a problem. Suppose you are going to make French bread. The recipe says to measure out six cups of flour. Measure it where? Into a soup bowl? The recipe doesn't say where to put the flour, but common sense tells you that six cups of flour won't go into a

Besides being known for his pioneering efforts in artificial intelligence, John McCarthy invented LISP, the second-oldest computer programming language still in use.

soup bowl. Common sense says to put it into a big mixing bowl. Next the recipe says to add one tablespoon of salt and one tablespoon of sugar. Add them where? Common sense says to put them into the flour that is in the big mixing bowl.

Common sense is a mechanism that comes from our experiences. It is ordinary to us, but it is very difficult to program computers to have such common sense. Computers can be fed sets of instructions, but they cannot experience the world in the comprehensive way that a human being can. Some of McCarthy's latest work involves teaching computers how to navigate in three-dimensional space, which people do quite easily.

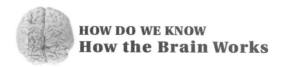
Herman Simon (1916–2001) was a cognitive scientist who came to the field from another area of research. Trained as an economist, he became interested in the decision-making process within large organizations. In 1952, he met Allen Newell, and the two men discovered that they shared the view that problem solving and decision making could be modeled using computer programs. Simon and others have given us insights on how people make decisions. He basically said that we rely on "rules of thumb." Our minds see patterns in situations and relate these patterns to experiences we have had. We make comparisons to determine if a particular pattern is completely similar to a stored pattern or if it has distinctive features. We evaluate the significance of what is unique in the new pattern and make a judgment about how it will affect the pattern. Decision making is the process that comes from judgment.

Another pioneer of cognitive science is the American linguist Noam Chomsky (1928–). Cognitive scientists study how language is acquired and represented in the brain and how the mind works when we use language. Language is a tool of the mind that we acquired by genetic and cultural evolution. As far as we know, only humans have language. Many other animals have communication systems, but these are not language, and attempts to teach language to non-humans have not really been successful.

In the 1960s, Chomsky helped linguists to break away from behavioral theory. He maintained that language arises only when an organism has reached a certain level of complexity, and he saw language ability as a biologically based, prewired feature of our brain. According to Chomsky, we are born with basic grammatical rules built into our neural networks, and these rules allow us to learn a language.

In other words, our brain is not like a blank slate just waiting to have grammatical rules and a growing vocabulary written on it. There's more to language than just vocabulary and rules of usage garnered from

Another way Noam Chomsky disproved behavioral theory is by stating that the mind has limited intercommunication and interaction with its other subsystems. For example, optical illusions cannot simply be turned off once known to be only illusions.

experience. From the very beginning, the mind knows that vocabulary has to have some sort of organization, and the brain has evolved built-in grammatical organizing patterns for the concepts, actions, and object-to-subject relationships described by language. Your brain is very smart and is ready to learn language as soon as you are old enough to speak. Not only is he a major force in linguistics, but Chomsky, who is originally from Philadelphia, is widely known for his political stance against U.S. foreign policy.

CONSCIOUSNESS

Consciousness is one of the most basic concepts we need to understand when we try to figure out how the mind works. It is what the mind is all about. The philosopher René Descartes said, "I think, therefore I am." Over the centuries, scholars have debated and drawn widely diverse conclusions from Descartes's statement, but he was really trying to make a very simple point. Philosophers known as idealists were questioning the reality of the world and the existence of the intelligent entities in it. Might not everything just be a dream in the mind of God? How could one prove that one existed? Descartes, a materialist philosopher, said that because he was self-aware, because he sensed himself thinking, he knew that he really existed.

Consciousness is the quality or state of being aware, especially of something within oneself. It is the highest level of mental life. One can only experience one's own consciousness with certainty, but it is reasonable to assume that other human beings experience the same sense of self-awareness. That seems evident from the way others speak to us. They talk about themselves as if they also experienced an inner mental life. The matter is not so simple with other species, however. Is your pet dog conscious in this sense? An animal can experience pain and pleasure. It can feel sad or happy. But is it aware of itself as a feeling or thinking creature? Can it have an abstract notion of itself as a member of a class of creatures ? No one is sure.

Consciousness is made up of many things. Much of it comes from an awareness of a continuous input of sensory information that makes us feel ourselves as separate from the rest of the world. Sensation and memory combine to create in ourselves a sense of a continuous existence over time. What would it be like to live without consciousness? We do live with some unconscious mental processes. We don't have to think about making our hearts beat or our lungs inhale or exhale, and when our finger touches a flame it draws back automatically, well before the pain signal reaches the brain. If all of our thought processes worked automatically this way, we could probably still survive as living creatures.

And for all we know, this is exactly how most nonhuman creatures go through life, reacting blindly to the sensation of the moment with no sense of being alive. But it is hard to imagine how creatures who possess language could live without self-awareness. Language encourages the capacity for generalization. When you can think about a class of objects rather than the one object before you at the moment, you are becoming conscious of the general character of objects in terms of abstract properties like color or shape. It is only a small step from this kind of

abstraction to thinking about yourself as a living being of a certain kind.

Explaining consciousness remains the ultimate goal of cognitive science and raises the profound question of whether the mind can ever know itself. Cognitive scientists are hard at work on the problem.

5

New Technologies in Brain Processes

Scientists are beginning to see the brain in action. They can watch a computer screen and observe a person's brain while that person is thinking, talking, or eating. Scientists do this with new imaging technologies.

At one time, studying the brain experimentally had to be limited to studying nonhuman

animals. Using rats, rabbits, cats, dogs, and monkeys, scientists would invade the brain, cutting out little pieces, hooking up electrical wires, and doing experiments to see how such actions affected the behavior of the animals. But scientists couldn't perform these experiments on living humans. Instead, they studied the human brain by autopsy after a person had died, as with the previously mentioned Tan. Scientists also learned much about how the human brain functions by studying the effects of strokes, brain tumors, and other injuries. Now, however, imaging technology has opened up a vast frontier of research possibilities using living subjects. Scientists are able to observe precisely how the brain processes information as it moves through the complex connections between nerve cells.

The first such technology to be developed was known as computerized tomography (CT) or computerized axial tomography (CAT). It was developed in the 1970s and is now used all over the world. The CAT scan, as it is commonly called, uses a beam of X-rays to take a cross-sectional picture of the brain, including the soft

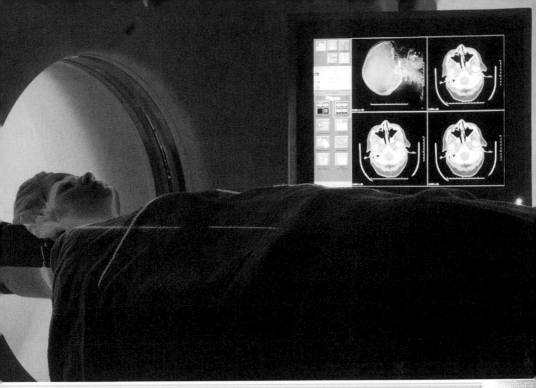

In a CAT scan, the platform upon which the patient lies slowly moves through the machine. The X-ray tube, on a movable ring at the edge of the hole, scans a narrow horizontal slice of the body with each revolution. After the patient has moved through the machine, all of the information is combined to give a detailed image.

tissues and blood vessels. The X-ray beam is mounted on a wheel that rotates around the subject. Because it is taking pictures from all angles, bones and other hard tissues do not block the view of the soft tissues in the final computer-assembled image. A dye, known as a contrast media, may be injected into the bloodstream to produce better images of areas of

concern to the scientist or physician. The computer can combine a number of these cross-sectional images into a multidimensional image of the brain or other internal organs.

In 1977, the first magnetic resonance imaging (MRI) scanner was developed by Dr. Raymond Damadian (1936–). Basically, the MRI scanner creates a strong magnetic field around the subject that forces spinning hydrogen atoms in the body's tissues to align themselves with the magnetic field. Pulses of radio waves at a special frequency then add energy to those hydrogen atoms, which are forced to spin in a slightly different direction. When these hydrogen atoms realign themselves with the magnetic field, they give off the extra energy, which can be detected and transformed into an image. Sometimes contrast media are injected for better images. MRI scanners are big, noisy, and uncomfortable, and they can be dangerous. Their magnets are so powerful that small metal objects like pens, keys, and paper clips can be pulled out of a subject's pockets to become flying projectiles. An MRI scanner can erase the magnetic encoding on a credit card. Heavier metal objects can be pulled right into the machine. But with proper preparation and caution, the MRI scan has proved very valuable in diagnosing illnesses and in studying the brain.

An advanced model of this device, called functional magnetic resonance imaging (fMRI), can recognize blood flow. When the brain is performing an activity like talking, more blood flows to the part of the brain that controls that activity. Along with this comes more oxygen, and that changes the radio emissions from the atoms in the tissues. This means that an fMRI scan can show which part of the brain is active when something is going on. This opens up a world of possibilities. For example, scientists can identify areas of brain tissue that are hyperactive in individuals suffering from various mental illnesses. They can observe what changes take place when they give a patient a certain antidepressant drug.

Another new imaging technique is called positron emission tomography (PET). Radioactive isotopes are injected into the subject, causing the brain to light up when it is thinking. Scientists can see the mind working in real time. The idea behind this approach is that brain cells burn glucose when they are functioning. If the glucose is tagged with radioactive atoms, it will burn stronger and brighter in the places where the brain is working harder. The PET scanner will pick this up and present it as a three-dimensional color picture. The brightest colors show the most intense mental activity. What actually happens is that the radioactive isotope gives off a positron, a tiny piece of antimatter. When this positron collides with an electron in the tissues of the brain, the two particles annihilate each other and give off a gamma ray, a very powerful electromagnetic pulse that can be detected by the scanner.

All these new technologies have come into being as a result of new discoveries in physics and computer science. Computers enable us to manipulate information

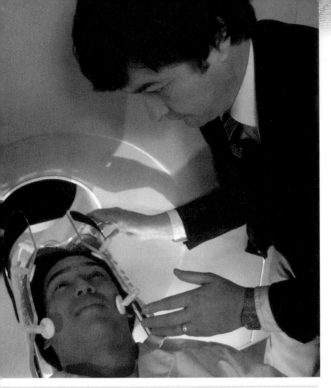

Dr. Michael Phelps, pictured here, developed the PET scan in 1973. Since it detects metabolic and chemical changes in the body, it is an effective technique for observing the effects of treatment.

digitally. We are not limited to the views provided by simple photographic processes. If we have the data, we can reconstruct an image from any angle or perspective, or we can combine data to form images that can be rotated or even turned inside out. And all of this can be done non-invasively, that is, without picking up a scalpel and damaging brain tissue.

By understanding the brain and the mind it produces, we can improve quality of life for all of us. There are more than 1,000 disorders related to the brain and the nervous system, with millions of people all over the world affected. The nature of health problems related

to the mind makes it urgent for us to understand its workings better. Researchers are seeking a better understanding of the causes of Alzheimer's disease, a progressive disease of the brain characterized by impairment of memory and other functions, such as language and perception. It is highly likely that deficient neurotransmitters are to blame. Autism is a condition characterized by difficulties in establishing normal social relations and strange and repetitive behavior. We have yet to fully understand brain tumors and illnesses like cerebral palsy, which affects our ability to initiate and control movements.

Epilepsy is another serious illness involving a malfunction in the firing of neurons. The firing rate may be four times the normal rate, causing an electrical storm in the brain and giving victims seizures. There are various hearing and vision disorders that originate not with the eyes and ears but deep inside the brain tissues. Multiple sclerosis is a disease of the central nervous system that destroys a person's control over bodily functions and leads to blindness and paralysis.

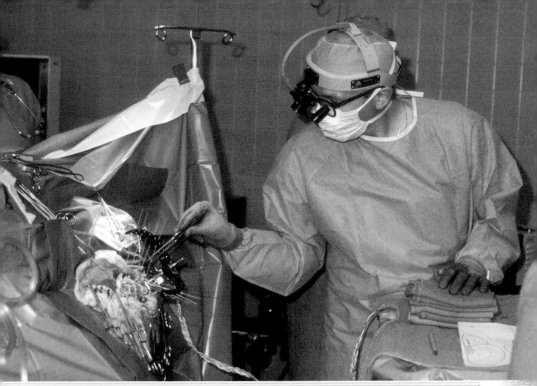

Although there is no cure for epilepsy, treatments include anti-epileptic drugs that control seizures, or, in some cases, surgery in which the small part of the brain is removed where the seizure takes place. Here, neurosurgeons are placing electrodes on an epileptic brain in an effort to locate where the seizures occur.

Parkinson's disease affects motor movement and gets progressively worse as the individual ages. Daily routine activities such as eating and bathing become difficult or impossible without help. Schizophrenia is a mental illness that causes loss of personality, strange behavior, withdrawal, and confusion. Strokes occur when brain cells are suddenly killed by a lack of oxygen because an

artery is blocked or ruptures. A number of different parts of the body may be paralyzed, depending on what part of the brain is involved. Dealing with all these illnesses will require further advances in medical technology and neuroscience.

THE FUTURE OF NEUROSCIENCE

Researchers have begun to look for the neural basis of sensations, emotions, and behavior. They are searching for the mind within the brain. They want to know what precise electrochemical changes occur when you get mad about something. We know a lot about how neurons work, how they communicate across synapses, and the chemical nature of neurotransmitters. But scientists have just barely started to understand how these physical elements produce thinking, feeling, senses, perceptions, and all that we associate with the mind and that make each of us a unique self.

We know that information is encoded by patterns of firing neurons, but we are not sure how these patterns make up the mind. How does a series of electrochemical switches translate into, for example, a feeling of affection? We understand how the brain handles motor activities, vision, hearing, speaking, and reflexes. But we have only just begun to understand such things as how a person's mental state can affect the immune system.

Although there are many unanswered questions, many amazing new developments are in the works. For example, engineers have developed devices that can be implanted in the brain that let sound bypass damaged parts of the inner ear and directly stimulate nerves that go into the brain, allowing the hearing impaired to recognize sounds. Artificial limbs are being connected to electronic sensors that allow the brain to control the movement of those limbs.

Another fascinating development is the brain pacemaker. We know about heart pacemakers because this technology has been around for a long time, and we might know some friend or family member who is successfully walking around with this device

implanted in his or her chest. Brain pacemakers are surgically implanted, like heart pacemakers. These devices send controlled impulses of electricity to specific areas of the brain. These impulses shut off the random, chaotic nerve signals that cause certain motor malfunctions, such as the tremors associated with Parkinson's disease.

Of particular importance to researchers is finding a way to enable neurons to regenerate themselves, as other cells in the body do. This would be a major step in restoring parts of the brain that have been damaged or destroyed. By generating new nerve tissue, we might cure various forms of paralysis and paraplegia. For a long time, scientists believed that the regeneration of nerve cells was not possible, but they are beginning to rethink this view. Perhaps by using embryonic stem cells, cells that have not yet developed into specialized tissues, we can repair neural pathways. Sperry Roger Wolcott (1913–1994) won the Nobel Prize in 1981 for his work in functional specialization in the cerebral hemispheres and the regeneration of nerve fibers.

NEW TECHNOLOGIES IN BRAIN PROCESSES

On July 17, 1990, President George H. W. Bush issued a proclamation establishing the 1990s as the "decade of the brain." In terms of new medical scanning technologies and the research accomplished, the 1990s truly were the decade of the brain. But even more exciting decades lie ahead. Our understanding of the brain is moving forward at a fast pace.

Glossary

autopsy The opening and examination of a dead body in order to discover the cause of death or the changes produced by disease.

awareness Self-knowledge of one's existence, or knowledge of something based on alertness, observation, and experience.

digital Referring to the property of information or measurements not expressed as a continuous range of values, but expressed in small, discrete units.

electrochemical Having to do with both electrical and chemical forces.

galvanometer An instrument that measures a small electrical current by movements of a magnetic needle.

gene The basic unit of heredity. Each cell has a complete set of all the genes that determine the characteristics of an organism.

glucose A type of sugar that supplies energy for biological processes.

imaging The use of specialized instruments and techniques to take pictures of the interior of the body.

linguistics The study of speech and language.

neurophysiology A branch of neuroscience that deals with the electrochemical functions of the nervous system.

nucleolus A small body inside a cell nucleus that is involved in the production of protein for the organism.

pathology The study of the causes and nature of disease.

perception Awareness of something through the senses, such as sight, hearing, smell, taste, and touch.

physiology A branch of science that deals with the normal functions of plants and animals while they are living.

radioactivity The emission of spontaneous radiation from an unstable atomic nucleus.

reflex An automatic physical reaction to a sudden stimulus.

regeneration The ability of damaged cells and tissues to grow again.

sensation Information received from the sense organs that allows an organism to apprehend the external physical world.

stochastic Involving a random variable.

For More Information

ORGANIZATIONS

American Association for Artificial Intelligence
445 Burgess Drive
Menlo Park, CA 94025-3442
(650) 328-3123
Web site: http://www.aaai.org

National Mental Health Association
2001 N. Beauregard Street, 12th Floor
Alexandria, VA 22311
(703) 684-7722
Resource Center: (800) 969-NMHA
Web site: http://www.nmha.org

MAGAZINES

Behavioral Brain Research

Customer Service Department

6277 Sea Harbor Drive

Orlando, FL 32887-4800

(877) 839-7126

e-mail: usjcs@elsevier.com

Neuropsychology

American Psychological Association

Subscriptions

750 First Street NE

Washington, DC 20002-4242

(202) 336-5600

WEB SITES

Due to the changing nature of Internet links, the Rosen Publishing Group, Inc., has developed an online list of Web sites related to the subject of this book. This site is updated regularly. Please use this link to access the list:

http://www.rosenlinks.com/gsq/hobw

For Further Reading

Asimov, Isaac. *How Did We Find Out About the Brain?* New York: Walker, 1987.

Brynie, Faith Hickman. *101 Questions Your Brain Has Asked About Itself But Couldn't Answer . . . Until Now.* Brookfield, CT: Millbrook Press, 1998.

How Things Work: The Brain. Alexandria, VA: Time-Life Books, 1990.

Johnston, Joni E. *The Complete Idiot's Guide to Psychology.* Indianapolis: Alpha Books, 2000.

Powledge, Tabitha M. *Your Brain: How You Got It and How It Works.* New York: Charles Scribner's Sons, 1994.

HOW DO WE KNOW
How the Brain Works

Sagan, Carl. *The Dragons of Eden: Speculations on the Evolution of Human Intelligence.* New York: Random House, 1979.

Wittrock, M. C. *The Human Brain.* Englewood Cliffs, NJ: Prentice Hall, 1977.

Bibliography

Bradley, P. B, ed. *Methods in Brain Research*. New York: Wiley, 1975.

Brady, Roscoe O., ed. *The Basic Neurosciences*. New York: Raven Press, 1975.

Singer, George, and Deborah Graham, eds. *Decade of the Brain*. Bundoora, Australia: La Trobe University Press, 1995.

Slaughter, Malcolm, ed. *Basic Concepts in Neuroscience: A Student's Survival Guide*. New York: McGraw-Hill, 2002.

Society for Neuroscience. *Brain Facts: A Primer on the Brain and Nervous System*. Washington, DC: Society for Neuroscience, 2002.

Index

Credits